The Sahara Desert

By Molly Aloian

🌳 Crabtree Publishing Company

www.crabtreebooks.com

Crabtree Publishing Company

www.crabtreebooks.com

Dedicated by Samara Parent
For Elliott and Nathan—Have fun in the sand!

Author: Molly Aloian
Publishing plan research and development:
  Sean Charlebois, Reagan Miller
  Crabtree Publishing Company
Editor and indexer: Wendy Scavuzzo
Design: Samara Parent
Photo research: Samara Parent
Project coordinator: Kathy Middleton
Print and production coordinator: Katherine Berti
Prepress technician: Samara Parent

Picture credits:
Dreamstime: page 13 (top left)
Istockphoto: pages 21 (top), 22 (top)
Shutterstock: cover, pages 1, 4, 7 (bottom), 8, 9 (both), 11, 12 (top), 13 (top middle right, top right and bottom), 14, 15, 16, 18, 19 (bottom), 20, 21 (bottom middle (both) and bottom right), 24, 26, 27; Attila JANDI: pages 6, 25
Thinkstock: pages 7 (top), 22 (bottom)
Wikimedia Commons: NOAA, US Gov, Unidentified: page 10; Alvesgaspar: page 12 (middle); Franzfoto: 12 (bottom); Hans Hillewaert: page 13 (top middle left); René Caillié: page 17; H. Krisp: page 19 (top); Chemicalinterest: page 21 (bottom left); Trekkingsinai: page 23

Library and Archives Canada Cataloguing in Publication

Aloian, Molly
    The Sahara Desert / Molly Aloian.

(Deserts around the world)
Includes index.
Issued also in electronic formats.
ISBN 978-0-7787-0714-1 (bound).--ISBN 978-0-7787-0722-6 (pbk.)

    1. Sahara--Juvenile literature. I. Title. II. Series: Deserts around the world (St. Catharines, Ont.)

DT334.A56 2012   j966   C2012-905678-2

Library of Congress Cataloging-in-Publication Data

CIP available at Library of Congress

Crabtree Publishing Company

www.crabtreebooks.com   1-800-387-7650

Printed in Canada/102012/MA20120817

Published in Canada
Crabtree Publishing
616 Welland Ave.
St. Catharines, Ontario
L2M 5V6

Published in the United States
Crabtree Publishing
PMB 59051
350 Fifth Avenue, 59th Floor
New York, New York 10118

Published in the United Kingdom
Crabtree Publishing
Maritime House
Basin Road North, Hove
BN41 1WR

Published in Australia
Crabtree Publishing
3 Charles Street
Coburg North
VIC 3058

CONTENTS

Words that are defined in the glossary are in
bold type the first time they appear in the text.

CHAPTER 1
The Sahara Desert

The Sahara is an enormous desert in Africa. It is the world's largest hot desert. It occupies nearly all of northern Africa, stretching from the Red Sea in the east to the Atlantic Ocean in the west. The Sahara covers 3.5 million square miles (9.1 million sq km), roughly the same size as the United States. It is one of the hottest places on the planet—temperatures have reached over 130°F (54°C). There are **plateaus**, shallow **basins**, mountains, and sand dunes in the Sahara, but barren gravel plains, called regs, cover the largest part of the desert.

The Tadrart region of the Sahara Desert is in the southeastern part of Algeria. It contains unusual rock formations and lofty sand dunes.

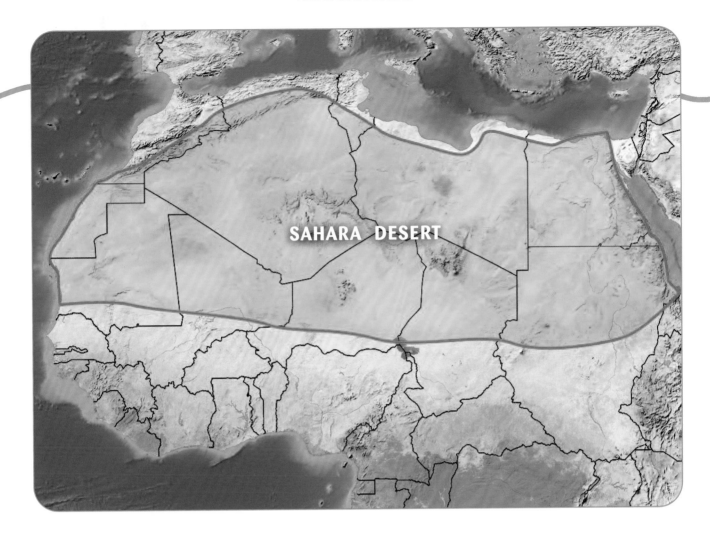

SAHARA DESERT

Sahara Sub-Climates

Many experts believe that the Sahara's climate is made up of two sub-climates. There is a dry subtropical climate in the north and a dry tropical climate in the south. In the dry subtropical zone, winters are cool, with an average temperature of 55°F (13°C). The summers are extremely hot. The highest temperature ever recorded was 136°F (58°C). Average rainfall in this region is about three inches (8 cm) per year. In the dry tropical zone, the average temperature is about 31.5°F (–0.3°C), but can drop as low as 5°F (–15°C) in the mountains. The average rainfall in this zone is about five inches (12.7 cm) per year. It sometimes snows in the higher elevations.

Survival Skills

Despite the dry, hot climate, several types of plants, including shrubs, grasses, cypress trees, and olive trees, manage to grow in the Sahara. Sahara desert animals include spotted hyenas, Dorcas gazelles, Cape hares, gerbils, jerboas, lizards, snakes, and hundreds of species of **migratory** birds. These plants and animals have **adapted** to the high temperatures and lack of rainfall and are able to survive in the Sahara.

Capable Camels

Camels are the main form of transportation for people and goods in the Sahara Desert. The camels in Africa are Arabian camels, also known as dromedaries. They have only one hump. These camels have bodies that are suited to life in the Sahara. They can walk across the desert for eight days without eating or drinking because they store fat in their humps. The camel can break the fat down into water and energy when food or water is not available. When water is available, camels can drink up to 30 gallons (114 liters) of water in a matter of minutes. They have long eyelashes and nostrils that can close to keep sand out of their eyes and nose. Big, fat footpads help the camels walk over rough, rocky terrain and shifting desert sands without sinking under their own weight. Camels also made it possible to establish trade routes across the Sahara, linking western Africa to northern Africa.

Desert People

People have lived in the Sahara Desert for thousands of years. Some **archeologists** believe that many more people lived in the Sahara thousands of years ago when the desert's climate was not as harsh and dry as it is today. They have found fossils, rock art, stone artifacts, bone harpoons, and other items in regions that are considered too hot and too dry for humans to inhabit today. Today, the majority of the people living in the Sahara Desert are **nomads**. The Tuareg and the Sahrawi are just two of the groups of nomads living in the Sahara Desert. The Tuareg live mainly in Algeria, Mali, Libya, and Niger and the Sahrawi live mainly in the western part of the desert.

This Tuareg man relies on his camel herd for survival. He must feed and care for the entire herd.

FAST FACT
In the Arabic language, the word "Sahrawi" means "of the Sahara."

Desert in Danger

There are factors threatening the health of the Sahara Desert and the health of the many plants, animals, and people that call the desert home. The desert is expanding at an alarming rate in a process called **desertification**. Experts estimate that the desert grows between three to six miles (5–10 km) per year. As desertification occurs, the few areas that can currently be used for farming become barren wastelands. The most environmental **degradation** is found in oases and other areas where there are small amounts of water available.

Umm al-Ma Lake is one of the group of about 20 Ubari Lakes in Libya. It is one of the most picturesque of the lakes.

Baobab trees can store hundreds of gallons (liters) of water in their huge trunks.

The Sahel

The Sahel is a region of semi-arid **steppes** along the southern edge of the Sahara, extending from Senegal eastward to Sudan. It is a **transitional** zone between the Sahara and the humid **savannahs** to the south. This unique region supports more life than the Sahara. Acacia and baobab trees, thorny shrubs, grasses, and other plants are found in the Sahel. There are also herds of cattle, goats, and sheep, and villages of people who tend food crops. In the 1970s, drought and famine killed nearly 200,000 people in the Sahel. Today, the area is threatened by **deforestation**, overpopulation, desertification, and drought.

CHAPTER 2

The Sahara Up Close

A desert can be defined in different ways, but many scientists believe that a desert is an area that receives less than 10 inches (25 cm) of rain per year. Most deserts are very hot, but some, such as the Gobi Desert, receive snow and are considered cold deserts. All deserts lose more moisture through evaporation than they receive from precipitation. They may seem to be barren wastelands, but deserts have formed over millions of years and contain a vast array of plants and animals that have adapted to the harsh conditions.

Sand dunes in the Libyan Sahara can reach over 1,640 feet (500 meters) high.

Changing Climate

In the last few hundred thousand years, the Sahara has undergone various climatic changes. For example, during the last glaciation, which began about 110,000 years ago and ended around 12,500 years ago, the Sahara was much bigger. There was even less precipitation in the area than there is today. From 8,000 B.C.E. to 6,000 B.C.E., the amount of rainfall in the Sahara increased because of low pressure over ice sheets to the north. After these ice sheets melted, the low pressure shifted and the northern Sahara dried out. The southern Sahara continued to receive moisture due to the presence of a **monsoon**.

Becoming a Grassland

During the next 500 years, the Sahara became a grassland region filled with trees, savannahs, and lakes. There were even large rivers, such as the Wadi Howar, which was once the largest tributary to the Nile River from the Sahara. Wildlife included elephants, rhinoceroses, hippopotamuses, crocodiles, and more than 30 species of fish. People also moved into the area. Researchers have used **radiocarbon dating** to determine the ages of human and animal remains from more than 150 **excavation** sites.

FAST FACT
The Sahara covers parts of several African countries including Algeria, Chad, Egypt, Libya, Mali, Mauritania, Morocco, Niger, Sudan, and Tunisia.

Dried Out Again

Climate change and the retreating monsoon rains caused temperatures to increase throughout the Sahara Desert and summers became longer and hotter once again. The monsoon shifted to the south and the desert began to dry out. Furthermore, the Intertropical Convergence Zone (ITCZ) in the southern Sahara prevents moisture from reaching the area. Storms to the north stop before reaching the desert.

In the Zone

The Intertropical Convergence Zone, or ITCZ, is the region that circles Earth, near the **equator**, where the trade winds in the Northern Hemisphere and Southern Hemisphere come together. The warm water and heat from the sun near the equator heats up the air in the ITCZ, raising its humidity and making it **buoyant**. As this buoyant air rises, it expands and cools, releasing the accumulated moisture in a series of continuous thunderstorms. These thunderstorms never reach the Sahara, however. In Africa, the ITCZ is located just south of the Sahel, so rain pours on the region south of the Sahara Desert.

Trees and grasses grow in the Sahel region of Africa because it receives more rain than the regions to the north.

Where's the Water?

Today, the only permanent river in the desert is the Nile River that flows from central Africa to the Mediterranean Sea. Other water in the Sahara is found in underground **aquifers**. In areas where this water reaches the surface, there are oases and there may be small towns or settlements such as the Bahariya Oasis in Egypt and Ghardaïa in Algeria. Oases are places in the desert where underground water rises to the surface. Oases cover only about 800 square miles (2,072 sq km) of the Sahara Desert and about 75 percent of the people in the Sahara live in or near these oases. Nomadic peoples use oases as places to rest and replenish food and water supplies.

FAST FACT
There are several wadis in the Sahara Desert in Egypt. Wadis are dry riverbeds that fill with water during rainfall.

The Ahaggar Mountains are in the central part of the Sahara Desert in southern Algeria. People have discovered ancient cave paintings in parts of the mountain range.

Desert Mountains

There are mountain ranges within the Sahara. The Ahaggar Mountains, or Hoggar Mountains, are in southern Algeria. The range's tallest peak, Mount Tahat, is 9,853 feet (3,003 meters) high. The range is composed mainly of volcanic rock. The Aïr Mountains are in northern Niger. They rise to more than 6,000 feet (1,829 m) and extend over 32,000 square miles (82,880 sq km). Mount Emi Koussi is the highest peak in the Sahara Desert. It is 11,204 feet (3,415 m) high and is part of the Tibesti Mountains in northern Chad.

Sahara Desert Plants

Most of the plants in the Sahara Desert live along the northern and southern parts of the desert and near the oases. Many plants have long roots that reach far down into the ground to absorb as much water as possible. The thick bark and waxy leaves on desert trees help the trees conserve water. Thick stems also allow the plants to store water. In the drier parts of the Sahara, the seeds of flowering plants sprout very quickly after it rains. They grow shallow roots and complete their growing cycle in just a few days before the soil dries out again. The new seeds the plants produce may lie **dormant** in the dry soil for years, waiting for the next rainfall. Other plants have networks of roots that spread out just under the surface of the ground. These roots absorb any water immediately after it has rained. Common desert plants include cypress trees, olive trees, acacia trees, doum palm, date palm, thyme, oleander, and certain types of grasses.

This extremely rare Saharan cypress is growing in Tassili n'Ajjer National Park. Saharan cypresses are also among the world's oldest trees. Some are more than 3,000 years old.

Oleanders (Nerium oleander) grow only in a few places in the Sahara Desert.

The fruit from date palm trees have been an important food in North Africa for hundreds of years.

FAST FACT
The doum palm is also known as the gingerbread palm. Its reddish-orange, apple-sized fruit tastes like gingerbread.

Keeping Cool

Sahara Desert animals include gerbils, jerboas, Cape hares, Dorcas gazelles, Barbary sheep, oryx, spotted hyenas, common jackals, and sand foxes. Reptiles such as frogs, toads, sand vipers, and monitor lizards live in the Sahara as well. During the scorching heat of the day, most animals remain inactive or stay underground in **burrows**, where the temperatures are cooler. They come out at night to search for food.

Jerboa

Oryx

Frog

Monitor Lizard

Amazing Acacia

Acacia trees grow primarily in wadis in the Sahara Desert. Wadis are temporary water sources created by rainfall. The acacia has a narrow, thin trunk, small feathery leaves, and numerous thorns. It is also fire resistant. When there is no rain, acacias may not produce leaves. People used the **resin** from acacia trees as ointment to treat wounds, and the leaves to make colors for paints.

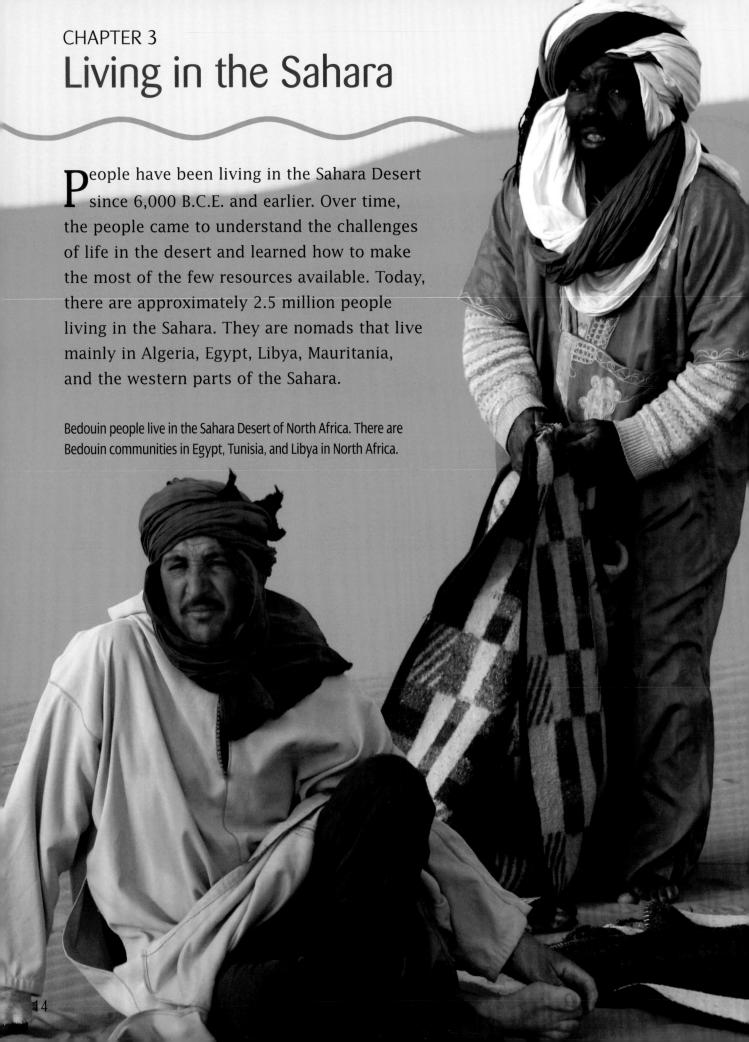

CHAPTER 3
Living in the Sahara

People have been living in the Sahara Desert since 6,000 B.C.E. and earlier. Over time, the people came to understand the challenges of life in the desert and learned how to make the most of the few resources available. Today, there are approximately 2.5 million people living in the Sahara. They are nomads that live mainly in Algeria, Egypt, Libya, Mauritania, and the western parts of the Sahara.

Bedouin people live in the Sahara Desert of North Africa. There are Bedouin communities in Egypt, Tunisia, and Libya in North Africa.

This man and his camels are resting in an oasis in Morocco.

Life Long Ago

Long ago, before recorded history, there were many more people living in the Sahara. Archaeologists have discovered stone artifacts, fossils, and rock art in regions that are now much too dry for people or animals to live in. Bone harpoons, stone tools, shells, cave drawings and engravings, and fossils have been found in prehistoric settlements along the shores of ancient lakes in the Sahara. These artifacts show that humans, elephants, rhinoceroses, fish, crocodiles, antelopes, and many other animals once lived in what is now the Sahara Desert. Around 7,000 years ago, people were hunting, fishing, and raising herds of animals in the Sahara region. It is believed that groups of people from northeastern Africa brought sheep and goats into the Sahara. About 6,000 years ago, people in Egypt began growing crops of barley and wheat that may have been brought in from Asia.

NOTABLE QUOTE

"No man can live [in the desert] and emerge unchanged. He will carry, however faint, the imprint of the desert, the brand which marks the nomad; and he will have within him the yearning to return…"

—Wilfred Thesiger, *Arabian Sands*

Fennec Fox

The fennec fox is suited to life in the harsh Sahara Desert. It is the smallest fox in the world, but it has extremely large ears to **radiate** body heat and help keep it cool. Its ears are about 6 inches (15 cm) long. The fox also uses its oversized ears to pick up even the slightest sounds and locate prey at night. The fox emerges from its cooler burrow at night to hunt for beetles and rodents. The fox's long, thick fur helps to keep it warm during the chilly desert nights and protects it from the hot sun during the day. Furry feet help to protect the fox from the burning Sahara sand.

Ancient Trade

During these ancient times, there were many different groups of people living in the Sahara. The groups lived separately, but they often traded goods with one another. For example, copper from Mauritania had found its way to people in the Mediterranean during the Bronze Age by the 2nd millennium B.C.E. The Bronze Age was a time in early human history when people first began to make tools and weapons out of bronze. It occurred between the Stone Age and the Iron Age. Trade became even more common with the people of the Iron Age in the Sahara during the 1st century B.C.E., including the civilization centered in an ancient region in northeastern Africa called Nubia. Nubia was part of the Nile River Valley located in the southern part of present-day Egypt and in the northern part of present-day Sudan.

FAST FACT
According to today's estimates, there is only one person living in every square mile (2.6 sq km) of land in the Sahara.

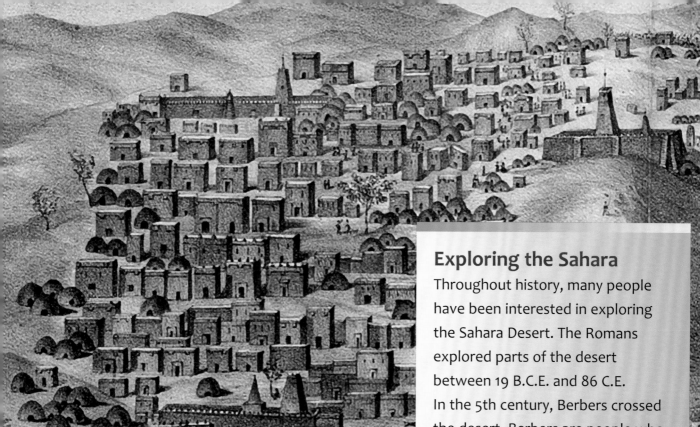

Trade Increases

Between the 7th and 11th centuries, **Islam** expanded into the present-day countries of Morocco, Algeria, Tunisia, and Libya and trade across the desert began to increase. Over time, people began traveling on established trade routes throughout the Sahara. Groups of nomads transported goods across the desert for trade. The groups traveled in caravans by camel and stopped at oases for food, water, and to rest. Gold, ivory tusks, ostrich feathers, leather, and other items reached Europe, where they became fashionable among wealthy Europeans. Trade throughout the Sahara linked the African **empires** of Ghana, Mali, and Songhay to eastern Africa and Europe. People from Sudan, which was part of the Ghana Empire, traded gold with Morocco and Algeria in exchange for salt.

Exploring the Sahara

Throughout history, many people have been interested in exploring the Sahara Desert. The Romans explored parts of the desert between 19 B.C.E. and 86 C.E. In the 5th century, Berbers crossed the desert. Berbers are people who have lived in northern Africa for thousands of years. Numerous Arab writers also described the Sahara in their texts. In 1798, a German explorer named Friedrich Hornemann traveled to the Sahara and joined a caravan heading across the northeastern part of the desert. The Scottish explorer Alexander Gordon Laing is famous for crossing the Sahara and reaching the mysterious city of Timbuktu in Mali in 1826. He was killed before he could return, however. The French explorer René Caillié managed to return from his visit to Timbuktu by crossing the Sahara from south to north in 1828. Caillié later wrote a book about his travels.

The drawing above depicts the city of Timbuktu in Mali, which René Caillié visited in 1828.

FAST FACT
At the age of 25, Tuareg men begin wearing a veil. The veil is a long strip of cotton, often dyed blue. The Tuareg are sometimes called "blue men" because of the blue veils they wear.

Desert Dwellers

When the Arab armies moved across northern Africa in the 11th century, they replaced the Berbers as the ruling population. Some of the Berbers were nomads. The most well-known of these nomads are the Tuareg. For centuries, the Tuareg have relied on herds of animals for survival in the desert. They traveled hundreds of miles across the desert searching for new grazing land for their herds of camels and goats. Tuareg camel caravans were extremely important in trans-Saharan trade until the mid-20th century. There were five main trade routes extending across the Sahara from the northern Mediterranean coast of Africa to the southern edge of the Sahara. Gold and spices were among the items traded and the Tuareg controlled all of the caravan trade routes.

Today, there are more than one million Tuareg living throughout the Saharan parts of Niger, Mali, Algeria, Libya, and Burkina Faso. The Tuareg call themselves Imohagh or Imajughen, which means "the noble people," in their language. Their language is called Tamashek, which is a language related to other North African languages. Some Tuareg have given up their nomadic way of life, and have settled in villages and towns. Others still live as nomads in their traditional ways.

Horned Viper

The horned viper is a sand-colored snake that lives in the Sahara Desert. It has a broad, triangular head and a horn that sticks out above each eye. The horned viper can burrow quickly into the sand by rapidly moving its body from side to side. Once it is concealed, the snake can ambush rodents, birds, and other animals. If loose sand is not available, the snake will hide under a rock or in the burrow of another animal.

(above) The desert horned viper is usually slightly less than two feet (0.6 m) in length. Its brownish-yellow color matches the sand so the snake can go unnoticed when hunting prey.

Sahara Salt

In the Sahara, salt is found in only a few places. People and animals need salt to survive, which makes it a very valuable commodity. Salt is also used to preserve and flavor food. For hundreds of years, Tuareg nomads used camel caravans to transport salt for trade. In Niger, Tuareg caravans continue to cross the desert to get salt from the Bilma oasis for trade. The salt is packed into various shapes, such as cones or flat cakes, depending on its origin and its quality.

(below) This camel caravan is hauling loads of salt to Timbuktu. The camels must rest after a long day of traveling.

CHAPTER 4
Tourism and Natural Resources

Nearly one million people travel to the Sahara Desert each year for tours, wildlife viewing, and safaris. Various **natural resources** are also found in the Sahara Desert. Tourism and natural resources have contributed somewhat to the economic development of villages and small communities in certain parts of the Sahara, but hundreds of thousands of local people are still struggling to survive throughout the desert.

Some tourists want to trek across the desert in camel caravans. They travel all day and camp overnight in desert oases.

FAST FACT
Tourism is an important part of the Moroccan economy. Tourism provides jobs for more than 250,000 people in Morocco.

Tourism

Many people visit the Sahara Desert to take in the spectacular landscapes, rare wildlife, and to better understand this harsh but unique part of the world. Some travel to the desert to participate in treks along with camel caravans. Desert areas in Tunisia and Morocco are popular tourist destinations, and tours in Algeria and Libya are gaining in popularity. Tourists flock to visit the Ahaggar Mountains in southern Algeria. **Paleontologists** and archaeologists in search of buried bones and other remnants from ancient peoples are also drawn to the Sahara Desert.

The male agama lizard develops colorful markings during breeding season. The head and neck turn bright orange and the body turns bright blue.

Minerals in the Sahara

Oil was discovered in the Sahara Desert after World War II. There are large reserves of oil in Libya and Algeria. In fact, more than 90 percent of export earnings in Libya and Algeria come from oil. Tunisia and Egypt also have oil reserves, but on a much smaller scale. Other mineral resources are major contributors to the economies of some Saharan countries.

Phosphates are Tunisia's main mineral export. There are several major deposits of iron in Algeria. There are substantial amounts of copper in southwestern Mauritania. There are also deposits of **uranium** in the Sahara, a metallic element that has been particularly important to the economy in Niger.

Magnesium Phosphate

Iron

Copper

Uranium

21

Prehistoric Paintings

Many tourists travel to Algeria's Tassili n'Ajjer National Park to see prehistoric rock paintings. Tassili n'Ajjer is a vast mountainous region in southeast Algeria at the borders of Libya and Niger. It covers an area of 27,799 square miles (72,000 sq km). There are more than 15,000 drawings and engravings in Tassili n'Ajjer. The drawings depict changes in climate, animal migrations, and what human life was like on the edge of the Sahara thousands of years ago. The rock art was discovered in 1933 and Tassili n'Ajjer was declared a UNESCO World Heritage Site in 1982.

Ancient Water

With so little rain in the Sahara, groundwater is a very important resource in the Sahara. Much of the groundwater in the Sahara is rich in nutrients and minerals and is suitable for growing crops and for **domestic** use. More than half of all the available groundwater is ancient water, however. It fell as rain thousands of years ago. The deepest water is hundreds of thousands of years old. The water above 1,600 feet (488 m) is about 160,000 years old. Once these water resources are used, they will not replenish until the next wet period in the Sahara, which might not occur for thousands of years.

(left) This rock engraving was found at an archaeological site called Wadi Mathendous. It is a UNESCO World Heritage Site in Libya.

Sahara Scorpions

Four of the Sahara's scorpion species are deadly to humans. In humans, the venom from these scorpions can cause temporary paralysis, convulsions, cardiac arrest, or respiratory failure. Some species have venom as toxic as the venom of a cobra. Most scorpions in the Sahara are active at night and hunt mainly insects. But some of the larger species, which can grow up to 7.5 inches (19 cm) long, will attack rodents and small lizards. The scorpions absorb water from the flesh of their prey.

Sand Seas

Ergs or sand seas cover approximately one-third of the Sahara Desert. An erg is a broad, flat area of desert covered with windswept sand. In the Erg Issouane, some dunes are 400 feet (122 m) high. Some of the most spectacular sand seas are the Grand Erg Oriental and the Grand Erg Occidental in Algeria, the Idehan-Marzuk Dunes in Libya, and the great ergs in Egypt's Western Desert. The Western Desert is one of the driest parts of the Sahara. Some tourists visit the Sahara to sandboard down these ergs. A sandboard is like a snowboard for the sand. People hike up the ergs, then ride their boards down.

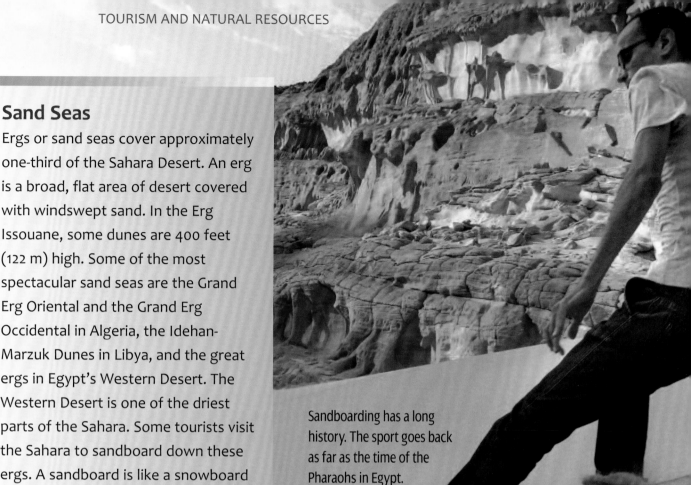

Sandboarding has a long history. The sport goes back as far as the time of the Pharaohs in Egypt.

N O T A B L E   Q U O T E

"Travelling in the Sahara Desert requires a major shift in perspective. The landscape is so vast that it's impossible to judge distance. The color palette—a thousand shades of greige—makes it hard to discern specific forms, and the intense sunlight reflecting off the sand tricks the eye into seeing things that don't exist. Self-reliance, otherwise an asset to travelers, is a potential liability: one mistake and you could vanish forever."

—John Vlahides, Lonely Planet Author

CHAPTER 5

The Sahara at Risk?

The Sahara Desert may appear to be inhospitable to the plants, animals, and people that live there, but the desert is actually extremely fragile. The unique plants and animals in the desert are constantly under threat from desertification, drought, and the activities of humans. Environmental organizations are starting to realize the need to protect the Sahara Desert and the plants, animals, and people living within it.

FAST FACT

In March 2012, the government of Niger officially established the Termit & Tin Toumma National Nature and Cultural Reserve. The 38,610 square mile (100,000 sq km) reserve is one of the largest single protected areas in Africa.

Desertification

Desertification is a serious problem in the Sahara and in the Sahel region of Africa. The causes of desertification in the driest parts of the world vary greatly from place to place. In some regions, desertification is the direct result of human activities. In other regions, the gradual change in climate causes the problem. In the Sahara and the Sahel region, clearing land for wood and cattle grazing are the two main factors leading to the spread of the desert.

This Peul woman lives in a village in Senossa, which is in southern-central Mali.

Pumping Problems

In recent years, development projects have brought Algeria and Tunisia water that is pumped from aquifers deep underground. The water is used for crops or drinking water. These types of projects might seem good at the time, but they often lead to soil degradation and **salinization** because of drainage problems. Furthermore, modern techniques used to pump water from underground sources dry up the groundwater reserves in a way that is irreversible.

Sahel Crisis

The lives of millions of people are threatened by drought in the Sahel region of Africa. There is significant rainfall only about once per year in the Sahel. The rains are sometimes late and do not cover the entire region. This is a disaster for the people, plants, and animals living there. The people live on what they can grow, so, when the rains do not arrive on time, harvests fail, animals die, and people go hungry. Drought is affecting people in parts of Chad, Niger, Mali, Mauritania, Berkina Faso, Senegal, Gambia, Cameroon, and northern Nigeria.

The addax is a slow-walking animal and is easy for predators and human hunters to catch.

Sahara Conservation Fund

The Sahara Conservation Fund or SCF is an organization dedicated to the conservation of the wildlife of the Sahara and the grasslands of the Sahel. The SCF's goal is a well-conserved Sahara Desert in which ecological processes function naturally, and plants and animals exist in healthy balance with one another. The SCF works with governments, international conventions, zoo communities, scientific communities, non-governmental organizations, and other agencies to help conserve the Sahara and other deserts and their natural and cultural heritage.

Critically Endangered Addax

The addax is a large antelope with short legs and long, corkscrew horns. It is well adapted to living in the desert. Large hooves help it move efficiently across shifting sands. It has a pale coat and gets all the water it needs from the plants it eats. In the hottest weather, the addax rests during the day and grazes at night and in the early morning. It uses its short, blunt muzzle to eat coarse desert grasses. When grasses are not available, it grazes on acacias, herbs, and water-rich plants such as tubers. The addax was once found all across North Africa. But over-hunting since the mid-1800s wiped out the large herds. The addax is now critically endangered, with fewer than 300 animals left in the wild.

International Year of Deserts and Desertification

The United Nations General Assembly declared the year 2006 the International Year of Deserts and Desertification. The assembly's goal was to spread awareness about the desert areas of the world and about the problem of desertification. It wants people to understand the importance of these natural habitats and the incredibly diverse plants and animals living there. The International Year of Deserts was designed to encourage people to celebrate the fragile beauty and unique heritage of the world's deserts and to show people that deserts deserve our protection.

There are many unusually shaped sandstone cliffs in Algeria's Tassili n'Ajjer.

NOTABLE QUOTE

"To the desert go prophets and hermits; through deserts go pilgrims and exiles. Here the leaders of the great religions have sought the therapeutic and spiritual values of retreat, not to escape but to find reality."

—Paul Shepard, *Man in the Landscape: A Historic View of the Esthetics of Nature*

COMPARING THE WORLD'S DESERTS

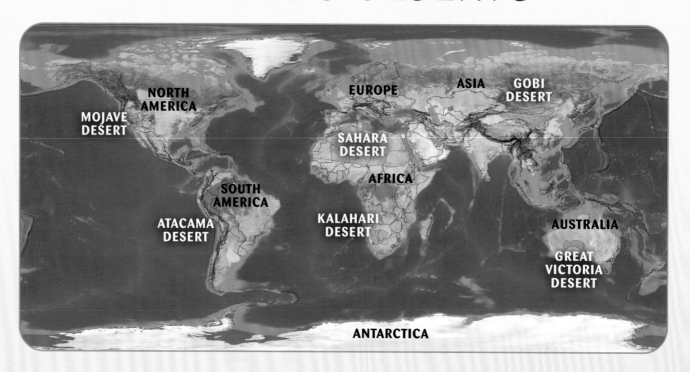

	Continent	Approximate Size	Type of Desert	Annual Precipitation	Natural Resources
Atacama	South America	40,600 square miles (105,154 sq km)	coastal desert	0.04 inches (1 mm)	copper, sodium nitrate, salt, lithium
Gobi	Asia	500,000 square miles (1,294,994 sq km)	cold desert	2–8 inches (5–20 cm)	oil, coal, copper, gold, petroleum, salt
Great Victoria	Australia	161,700 square miles (418,800 sq km)	hot, dry desert	8–10 inches (20–25 cm)	gold, opal, iron ore, copper, coal, oil
Kalahari	Africa	275,000 square miles (712,247 sq km)	semi-arid desert, arid savannah	5–25 inches (13–64 cm)	coal, copper, nickel, and diamonds
Mojave	North America	25,000 square miles (64,750 sq km)	hot, dry desert	2–6 inches (5–15 cm)	copper, gold, solar power
Sahara	Africa	3.5 million square miles (9.1 million sq km)	hot, dry desert	3 inches (8 cm)	coal, oil, natural gas, various minerals

TIMELINE

22,000–10,500 years ago	No people living outside of the Nile Valley; the Sahara Desert extended 250 miles (402 km) further south than it does today
10,500–6,000 years ago	Monsoon rains begin in the Sahara Desert, transforming it into a more lush area suitable for humans; Nile Valley dwellers settle in the region
9,000–7,300 years ago	Well-established human settlements in the Sahara Desert as a result of continued rains, vegetation growth, and animal migrations
7,300–5,500 years ago	Monsoon rains begin to retreat, desert conditions return in the Sahara
19 B.C.E.–86 C.E.	Romans explore parts of the Sahara
5th century	Berbers from North Africa cross the Sahara
11th–15th century	Goods are exported to Europe, Arabia, India, and China across the Sahara Desert
1798	German explorer Friedrich Hornemann travels to the Sahara
1826	Scottish explorer Alexander Gordon Laing crosses the Sahara and reaches the city of Timbuktu; he dies before returning
1828	French explorer René Caillié returns from his visit to Timbuktu by crossing the Sahara from south to north
1936–75	Most of the Saharan states achieve independence
2004	Sahara Conservation Fund is established
2006	United Nations General Assembly declares 2006 the International Year of Deserts and Desertification
2012	Government of Niger established the Termit & Tin Toumma National Nature Reserve

GLOSSARY

adapted Changed to fit a new or specific use or situation

aquifers Areas underground that hold water in the gaps between rock, sand, or gravel

archaeologists People who study past human life through fossils

basins Areas of land drained by a river and its tributaries

buoyant Able to float

burrows Holes in the ground made by animals for shelter or protection

climate change A long-term, lasting change in the weather conditions in an area

deforestation The action or process of clearing an area of forests

degradation The act or process of wearing something down by erosion

desertification The gradual development of desert-like conditions

domestic Relating to a home or household

dormant Not active

empires Major political divisions with large territories or peoples under one ruler with complete authority

equator The imaginary circle around the middle of Earth

excavation The process of uncovering by digging away soil

Islam A religion or faith based on God's messages to the prophet Muhammad

migratory Describing animals that move from one country, area or place to another for feeding or breeding

monsoon A seasonal wind in southern Asia that brings very heavy rainfall

natural resources Materials found in nature that are valuable or useful to humans

nomads People that have no permanent homes, but move from place to place throughout the year

paleontologists Scientists who study the life of past geologic periods through fossil remains

phosphates Salts of phosphoric acids

plateaus Flat areas of high land

prehistoric Relating to or existing in times before written history

radiate To emit or send out

radiocarbon dating A chemical process used to determine the age of archaeological materials through their radioactive carbon-14 content

resin A yellow or brownish substance found in trees

salinization The accumulation of salt

savannahs Rolling grasslands that contain scattered trees and shrubs

steppes Vast areas of land that are dry, flat, and covered with short grasses, shrubs, and trees

transitional Changing from one type of land to another

uranium A radioactive metallic element

FIND OUT MORE

BOOKS

Gaff, Jackie. *I Wonder Why the Sahara Is Cold at Night and other questions about deserts.* Kingfisher, 2004.

Kalman, Bobbie, and Rebecca Sjonger. *Explore Africa* (Explore the Continents). Crabtree Publishing Company, 2007.

Lappi, Megan. *The Sahara Desert: The Largest Desert in the World* (Natural Wonders). Weigl Publishers, 2006.

Wientraub, Aileen. *The Sahara Desert: The Biggest Desert* (Great Record Breakers in Nature). Powerkids Press, 2001.

WEBSITES

Encyclopedia of Earth—Sahara Desert
www.eoearth.org/article/Sahara_desert?
  topic=49460

WWF—Deserts
http://wwf.panda.org/about_our_earth/
  ecoregions/about/habitat_types/habitats/
  deserts/

SCF—Sahara Conservation Fund
www.saharaconservation.org/

Tassili National Park
www.archmillennium.net/
  tassili_national_park.htm

INDEX